Quality-Assurance Data for Routine Water Analyses by the U.S. Geological Survey Laboratory in Troy, New York— July 2003 through June 2005

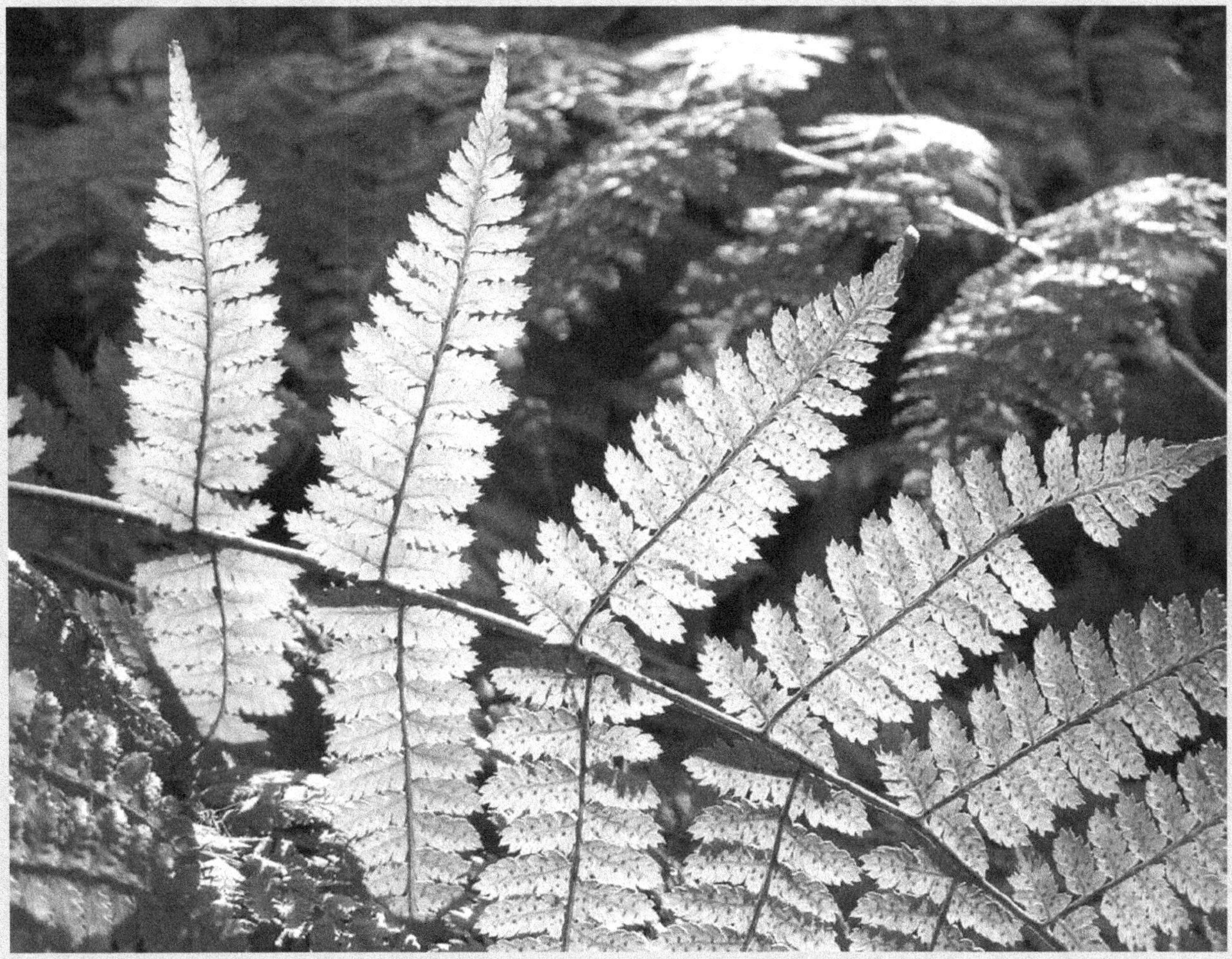

Open-File Report 2009–1233

U.S. Department of the Interior
U.S. Geological Survey

Cover.   Fern along access road near Bog Lake, Robinwood Park Club, western Adirondack State Park, Town of Long Lake, Hamilton County, New York ©2006 Peter deVries

Quality-Assurance Data for Routine Water Analyses by the U.S. Geological Survey Laboratory in Troy, New York— July 2003 Through June 2005

By Tricia A. Lincoln, Debra A. Horan-Ross, Michael R. McHale, and Gregory B. Lawrence

Open-File Report 2009–1233

U.S. Department of the Interior
U.S. Geological Survey

U.S. Department of the Interior
KEN SALAZAR, Secretary

U.S. Geological Survey
Marcia K. McNutt, Director

U.S. Geological Survey, Reston, Virginia 2009

For more information on the USGS—the Federal source for science about the Earth,
its natural and living resources, natural hazards, and the environment:
World Wide Web: http://www.usgs.gov
Telephone: 1–888–ASK–USGS

Suggested citation:
Lincoln, T.A., Horan-Ross, D.A., McHale, M.R., and Lawrence, G.B., 2009, Quality-assurance data for routine water
analyses by the U.S. Geological Survey laboratory in Troy, New York—July 2003 through June 2005: U.S. Geological
Survey Open-File Report 2009–1233, 34 p., available only at http://pubs.usgs.gov/of/2009/1233/.

Contents

Figures

Tables

Conversion Factors and Abbreviations

Multiply	By	To obtain
Length		
centimeter (cm)	0.3937	inch (in.)
Volume		
liter (L)	33.82	ounce, fluid (fl. oz)

Abbreviated Units of Measurement

mq/L	milligrams per liter
µeq/L	microequivalents per liter
µmol/L	micromoles per liter
µS/cm	microsiemens per centimeter
µg/L	micrograms per liter

Other Abbreviations

ANC	Acid-neutralizing capacity
AV	Analyzed value
CV	Coefficient of variation
D	Percent Difference
DI	Deionized Water
DOC	Dissolved organic carbon
DQO	Data-quality objective
MCV	Mean concentration value
MPV	Most probable value
NWRI	National Water Research Institute
QA	Quality assurance
QC	Quality Control
QC-high	High-concentration quality-control sample
QC-low	Low-concentration quality-control sample
SRS	Standard Reference Sample
TV	Troy Laboratory value
USGS	U.S. Geological Survey

Quality-Assurance Data for Routine Water Analyses by the U.S. Geological Survey Laboratory in Troy, New York— July 2003 Through June 2005

By Tricia A. Lincoln, Debra A. Horan-Ross, Michael R. McHale, and Gregory B. Lawrence

Abstract

The laboratory for analysis of low-ionic-strength water at the U.S. Geological Survey (USGS) Water Science Center in Troy, N.Y., analyzes samples collected by USGS projects throughout the Northeast. The laboratory's quality-assurance program is based on internal and interlaboratory quality-assurance samples and quality-control procedures that were developed to ensure proper sample collection, processing, and analysis. The quality-assurance and quality-control data were stored in the laboratory's Lab Master data-management system, which provides efficient review, compilation, and plotting of data. This report presents and discusses results of quality-assurance and quality control samples analyzed from July 2003 through June 2005.

Results for the quality-control samples for 20 analytical procedures were evaluated for bias and precision. Control charts indicate that data for five of the analytical procedures were occasionally biased for either high-concentration or low-concentration samples but were within control limits; these procedures were: acid-neutralizing capacity, total monomeric aluminum, pH, silicon, and sodium. Seven of the analytical procedures were biased throughout the analysis period for the high-concentration sample, but were within control limits; these procedures were: dissolved organic carbon, chloride, nitrate (ion chromatograph), nitrite, silicon, sodium, and sulfate. The calcium and magnesium procedures were biased throughout the analysis period for the low-concentration sample, but were within control limits. The total aluminum and specific conductance procedures were biased for the high-concentration and low-concentration samples, but were within control limits.

Results from the filter-blank and analytical-blank analyses indicate that the procedures for 17 of 18 analytes were within control limits, although the concentrations for blanks were occasionally outside the control limits. The data-quality objective was not met for dissolved organic carbon.

Sampling and analysis precision are evaluated herein in terms of the coefficient of variation obtained for triplicate samples in the procedures for 18 of the 22 analytes. At least 85 percent of the samples met data-quality objectives for all analytes except total monomeric aluminum (82 percent of samples met objectives), total aluminum (77 percent of samples met objectives), chloride (80 percent of samples met objectives), fluoride (76 percent of samples met objectives), and nitrate (ion chromatograph) (79 percent of samples met objectives). The ammonium and total dissolved nitrogen did not meet the data-quality objectives.

Results of the USGS interlaboratory Standard Reference Sample (SRS) Project indicated good data quality over the time period, with ratings for each sample in the satisfactory, good, and excellent ranges or less than 10 percent error. The P-sample (low-ionic-strength constituents) analysis had one marginal and two unsatisfactory ratings for the chloride procedure. The T-sample (trace constituents) analysis had two unsatisfactory ratings and one high range percent error for the aluminum procedure. The N-sample (nutrient constituents) analysis had one marginal rating for the nitrate procedure.

Results of Environment Canada's National Water Research Institute (NWRI) program indicated that at least 84 percent of the samples met data-quality objectives for 11 of the 14 analytes; the exceptions were ammonium, total aluminum, and acid-neutralizing capacity. The ammonium procedure did not meet data quality objectives in all studies. Data-quality objectives were not met in 23 percent of samples analyzed for total aluminum and 45 percent of samples analyzed acid-neutralizing capacity.

Results from blind reference-sample analyses indicated that data-quality objectives were met by at least 86 percent of the samples analyzed for calcium, chloride, fluoride, magnesium, pH, potassium, sodium, and sulfate. Data-quality objectives were not met by samples analyzed for fluoride.

Introduction

The U.S. Geological Survey (USGS) maintains a laboratory at its Water Science Center in Troy, N.Y., to analyze low-ionic-strength water for USGS watershed-research projects that require major-ion analyses of precipitation, soil-water, shallow groundwater, and stream-water samples. The methods used in this laboratory are described in detail in Lawrence and others (1995). Quality-assurance (QA) and quality-control (QC) data were collected, stored, and reviewed through the laboratory's Lab Master information management system during this report period.

The 22 analytes represented by this study were: acid-neutralizing capacity (ANC), total monomeric aluminum, organic monomeric aluminum, total aluminum, ammonium, boron, calcium, dissolved organic carbon (DOC), chloride, fluoride, magnesium, nitrate (ion chromatograph), nitrate (colorimetric method), nitrite, total dissolved nitrogen, pH, potassium, silicon, sodium, specific conductance, sulfate, and turbidity.

Purpose and Scope

This report documents the QA practices and QC data of this laboratory and is intended for use by cooperating agencies. It (1) describes QC and QA procedures of the laboratory; (2) presents graphs showing the results from analyses of QC samples, filter blanks and analytical blanks, triplicate environmental samples, interlaboratory QA samples, and blind reference samples; and (3) describes analytical biases and outliers and the corrective actions taken.

Participating Projects

The numbers and types of samples analyzed by the laboratory during the 2-year period are summarized below, by the project for which they are associated.

Project: Biogeochemical Processes that Control Nitrogen Cycling and Associated Hydrogen and Aluminum Leaching in an Undeveloped Headwater Basin
Cooperator: New York City Department of Environmental Protection
Analyses: 2,988 samples (stream water, shallow groundwater, soil-water solution, soil-water by expulsion method, and snow).

Project: Long-Term Monitoring of Five Streams in the Catskill Mountains
Cooperator: U.S. Environmental Protection Agency
Analyses: 697 stream-water samples.

Project: The Effects of the Clean Air Act on Water Quality of Medium-Scale Rivers in the Northeastern United States
Cooperator: U.S. Geological Survey, Office of Water Quality
Analysis: 252 stream-water samples.

Project: Adirondack Effects Assessment Program
Cooperator: Rensselaer Polytechnic Institute
Analyses: 484 stream-water samples.

Project: Upper and Lower Node Water-Quality Operation and Maintenance in the Catskill Mountains, New York
Cooperator: New York City Department of Environmental Protection
Analyses: 1,263 stream-water samples.

Project: Neversink River Natural Resources Study
Cooperator: The Nature Conservancy
Analysis: 25 stream-water samples.

Project: Collaborative Environmental Monitoring and Research Initiative
Cooperator: U.S. Geological Survey, Office of Water Quality and U.S. Forest Service
Analyses: 1,451 stream-water samples.

Project: Catskill Stream Restoration Study
Cooperator: New York City Department of Environmental Protection
Analyses: 71 stream-water samples.

Project: Potential Recovery of Water Chemistry in Stream Biota from Reduced Levels of Acid Deposition at a Sensitive Watershed in the Catskill Mountains
Cooperator: New York Energy Research and Development Authority
Analyses: 31 stream-water samples.

Additional information on projects of the New York Water Science Center is given in at *http://ny.water.usgs.gov*.

Quality-Assurance/Quality-Control (QA/QC) Program

The quality of the data produced at this laboratory is maintained by adherence to the standard operating procedures described in Lawrence and others (1995) and by participation in externally administered QA programs. Results of QA data are evaluated by the laboratory supervisor and primary analysts, and appropriate corrective action is taken when needed. The data-quality objectives (DQOs) are based on (1) the precision and accuracy levels generally required by projects that use the Troy Laboratory, and (2) the analytical limits of the methods used.

Quality-Control Samples

QC samples are used to measure the accuracy of an instrument's calibration and to detect variations in instrument response within an analytical run. Source material for all QC samples either is obtained from a manufacturer other than the producer of the source material used to make calibration standards or is obtained from a lot other than the source material used to make calibration standards.

The concentrations of QC samples are chosen to bracket the expected range of the environmental sample concentrations. A high-concentration QC sample and a low-concentration QC sample (referred to herein as QC-high and QC-low respectively) are prepared for most analyses; exceptions are inorganic monomeric aluminum, for which column efficiency is used to determine the acceptability of the data, fluoride, for which only one mid-level QC sample is prepared because the concentrations encountered by the laboratory are within a narrow range, and turbidity, for which a second set of calibration standards is checked against the daily calibration response factor of the instrument.

QC-high and QC-low samples are analyzed within a run for most constituents, exceptions are ANC, pH, and specific conductance. Either the QC-high sample or the QC-low sample is analyzed within an ANC, pH, and specific conductance run, depending upon the expected concentration range of the environmental samples.

QC samples are analyzed immediately after instrument calibration, after every 10 analyses of environmental samples, and at the end of each run. QC samples that do not meet DQOs for accuracy are rerun, and if the value is acceptable, the run is continued. If the rerun QC sample value is unacceptable, the environmental-sample data preceding it are considered to be out-of-control, the data are rejected, and the instrument is recalibrated. Only accepted QC-sample and environmental-sample data are entered into the database. An exception to this practice occurs when the volume of an environmental sample is insufficient for a rerun, in this case the environmental sample and QC data are entered into the database and flagged, and the project chief then decides whether to use or exclude these data from their reports. The analytical results of QC samples in this report indicate (1) the frequency of out-of-control data that are not rerun, and (2) biases and trends of control data. The numbers of samples analyzed and a summary of the QA data are given in table 1.

Filter Blanks and Analytical Blanks

A filter blank and an analytical blank are included in each group of 50 environmental samples.

Filter blanks are aliquots of deionized (DI) water that are processed and analyzed in the same manner as environmental samples. Filter blanks are analyzed only for constituents that require filtration. Filter-blank analysis indicates whether contamination has occurred during any step in sample handling, including bottle-washing procedures, filtration, sample preservation, or laboratory analysis.

Analytical blanks are aliquots of DI water that are processed and analyzed as environmental samples, except that the filtration step is omitted. Contamination found in analytical blanks may be attributed to any step in sample-handling, but not to filtration.

Table 1. Number of environmental and quality-control (QC) samples analyzed by the USGS Laboratory in Troy, N.Y., and summary of quality-control data for each constituent, July 2003 through June 2005.

[QC-high, high-concentration quality-control sample; QC-low, low-concentration quality-control sample]

Constituent	Number of samples analyzed			Number of QC samples exceeding control limits where environmental sample data are not rejected		Number of QC samples exceeding control limits by more than 5 percent where environmental sample data are not rejected	
	Environmental samples	QC-high samples	QC-low samples	QC-high	QC-low	QC-high	QC-low
Acid-neutralizing capacity	5,918	954	131	13	3	0	0
Aluminum, total monomeric	6,073	829	828	0	1	0	0
Aluminum, organic monomeric[1]	6,072	0	0	0	0	0	0
Aluminum, total	6,919	814	835	5	2	0	0
Ammonium	6,574	759	755	2	5	0	1
Boron	143	44	44	0	0	0	0
Calcium	6,021	707	688	1	0	0	0
Carbon, dissolved organic	6,432	868	871	5	18	0	2
Chloride	6,092	1,057	1,054	4	10	1	4
Fluoride	1,530	0	240	0	6	0	0
Magnesium	6,021	683	664	0	0	0	0
Nitrate (ion chromatography)	6,096	1,045	1,064	6	5	1	0
Nitrate (colorimetric method)	650	21	22	4	1	0	0
Nitrite	3,983	453	465	2	0	0	0
Nitrogen, total dissolved	3,380	473	474	0	7	0	3
pH	5,968	991	194	23	6	2	4
Potassium	5,990	734	732	0	0	0	0
Silicon	6,021	707	688	1	1	0	0
Sodium	6,000	717	717	1	0	0	0
Specific conductance	5,967	1,011	192	0	0	0	0
Sulfate	6,098	1,051	1,057	4	2	1	1
Turbidity[2]	540	0	0	0	0	0	0

[1]Column efficiency is used to determine the acceptability of the data.

[2]Comparison of standards to calibration response factor is used to determine the acceptability of the data.

Triplicate Environmental Samples

One set of triplicate environmental samples is included in each group of 50 samples. An environmental triplicate set consists of three consecutive samples collected at one field site. The purpose of environmental triplicate samples is to determine long-term analytical precision. Precision can be affected by bottle washing, sample-collection or sample-processing procedures, and analysis. Environmental samples are selected for triplicate analysis on a random basis to ensure a wide range of sample concentrations from several field sites. The laboratory alternates between analyzing a triplicate set consecutively and separating the triplicate set over a day or multiple day's analytical runs.

U.S. Geological Survey's Standard Reference Sample (SRS) Project

The USGS Standard Reference Sample (SRS) project conducts a national interlaboratory analytical evaluation program semiannually. The Troy Laboratory participates in the low-ionic-strength, nutrient, and trace components of this program. Typically, the reference samples consist of snow, rain, surface water, or deionized water that is collected, filtered, and possibly spiked with reagent-grade chemicals to meet the goals of the program. Reference samples for low-ionic-strength constituents are prefixed by a P and are analyzed for calcium, chloride, magnesium, pH, potassium, sodium, specific conductance, and sulfate. Reference samples for nutrient constituents are prefixed by an N and are analyzed for ammonium and nitrate. Reference samples for trace constituents are prefixed by a T and are analyzed for aluminum, calcium, magnesium, potassium, silicon, and sodium. Laboratory personnel are aware of the presence of the SRS sample at the time of analysis but do not know the constituent concentrations until a published report is received from the USGS after the conclusion of each study. The most probable value (MPV) for each constituent is equal to the median value calculated from the results submitted by participating laboratories. Laboratory performance is rated numerically by comparing analysis results to the MPVs for each constituent; the highest score is 4.0, and the lowest is 0.0. Beginning with the evaluation program in the spring of 2005, laboratory results are compared to the MPV and a percent difference is calculated for each constituent. The SRS project discontinued use of the laboratory rating system.

National Water Research Institute Ecosystem Interlaboratory QA Program

The Troy Laboratory participates in Environment Canada's National Water Research Institute (NWRI) Ecosystem Interlaboratory QA program, in which a set of 10 samples is analyzed twice yearly. The samples are obtained from predominantly low-ionic-strength waters from several sources, such as precipitation, snow, lakes, and streams throughout North America. The concentrations of the constituents in the NWRI samples are similar to those of the environmental samples analyzed at the Troy Laboratory. Laboratory results are compared with a median concentration value (MCV) calculated from results from all participants in the NWRI program. Laboratory personnel are aware of the presence of NWRI samples at the time of analysis but do not know the MCV of the constituents until Environment Canada publishes a report at the conclusion of each study.

Blind Reference Samples

The Troy Laboratory disguises USGS SRS samples from previous studies as routine environmental samples. These blind reference samples are processed and analyzed as environmental samples and therefore appear to the analyst to be project samples. The blind reference samples have MPVs that were reported by the USGS SRS project. The SRS samples are rotated as supplies are exhausted, and periodically the identity of the blind reference sample is changed. One blind reference sample is included in each set of 50 environmental samples. The Troy Laboratory used SRS P-samples as the blind reference samples during the time period represented in this report.

Control-Chart Evaluation

Control charts (figs. 1–5) are plots of QC data through time. This report uses control charts to (1) indicate whether the laboratory DQOs are met for individual QC samples; (2) reveal long-term biases within and outside the control limits; and (3) provide comparisons with results from other laboratories.

Each analyte has prescribed control limits that have been established to meet project DQOs (table 2). A constituent analysis is considered biased if 70 percent or more of the points on a chart are above or below the target value.

Quality-Control Samples

QC sample analysis data are plotted on control charts (fig. 1) in which the central line is equal to the target value of the control sample. The control limits for the samples are represented by the upper and lower control-limit lines on each chart. QC-high and QC-low samples are plotted on separate graphs by constituent and date of analysis, and the control charts are evaluated for trends and (or) bias and precision. All data are reported in micromoles per liter (µmol/L) except for pH (pH units), ANC (microequivalents per liter, µeq/L), and specific conductance (microsiemens per centimeter, µS/cm).

Filter Blanks and Analytical Blanks

Results from the blank analyses are plotted on control charts by constituent in figure 2. The control limits are represented by horizontal lines on the control charts. Data are plotted as concentration in relation to date of collection. Negative blank concentrations are encountered frequently. During analysis the instrument calibration curve is extrapolated beyond the lowest standard in order to evaluate blank samples, and negative concentrations reflect the practical limitations of the extrapolation. An outlier on the control chart indicates possible contamination.

Triplicate Environmental Samples

The coefficient of variation (CV) for each triplicate sample concentration is plotted by constituent and date of collection in figure 3. Data with mean concentrations less than the defined reporting limit (table 2) are excluded. The DQO for all constituents is a CV of less than 10 percent, with the exception of ANC, total monomeric aluminum, organic monomeric aluminum, total aluminum, and ammonium, for which it is 15 percent. Each circle within the control charts represents the CV of a triplicate environmental sample.

$$CV = \frac{s}{\bar{X}}(100) \tag{1}$$

where s =   standard deviation,

and $\bar{X}$ =   arithmetic mean of triplicate samples.

The ANC data are plotted on two graphs. The first (fig. 3A1) shows the CV for triplicate sample means outside the range of ±20 µeq/L; the absolute value of the mean is used to calculate the CV. The second (fig. 3A2) shows values within ±20 µeq/L; each symbol on the second graph represents the difference between the triplicate sample mean and the individual values of that triplicate sample.

Table 2. Reporting limits and data-quality objectives (DQOs) for accuracy, precision, and blanks for solution analyses performed by the USGS Laboratory in Troy, N.Y., July 2003 through June 2005.

[ANC, acid-neutralizing capacity; CV, coefficient of variation; DQO, data-quality objective; µmol/L, micromoles per liter; QC, quality control]

| Constituent or property | Reporting limit (µmol/L) | Accuracy | | | | Precision | |
| | | Low-concentration QC sample | | High-concentration QC sample | | Environmental triplicate samples DQO (CV) | Filter and analytical blanks DQO (µmol/L) |
		DQO (percent error)	Concentration (µmol/L)	DQO (percent error)	Concentration (µmol/L)		
Acid-neutralizing capacity[1]	none	10	(-39.9)	10	(125)	15	none
Aluminum, total monomeric	1.5	15	7.41	10	18.5	15	1.0
Aluminum, organic monomeric[2]	1.5	none	none	none	none	15	1.0
Aluminum, total	1.0	15	1.49	10	11.2	15	1.0
Ammonium	2.0	15	7.14	10	17.9	15	1.5
Boron	1.0	10	3.70	10	18.5	10	1.0
Calcium	2.0	10	25.0	10	99.8	10	1.0
Carbon, dissolved organic[3]	41.0	15	83.3	10	416	10	18
Chloride	3.0	10	8.47	10	84.7	10	2.0
Fluoride	0.5	20	1.58	none	none	10	0.5
Magnesium	1.0	10	10.3	10	41.1	10	0.5
Nitrate (ion chromatography)	2.0	10	4.84	10	48.4	10	0.3
Nitrate (colorimetric method)	5.0	15	42.9	10	100	none	none
Nitrite	0.5	15	7.14	10	28.6	10	1.0
Nitrogen, total dissolved	10	20	21.4	10	100	10	2.0
pH[4]	none	10	(4.44)	20	(6.88)	10	none
Potassium	1.0	10	6.40	10	25.6	10	0.5
Silicon	6.0	10	35.6	10	107	10	3.0
Sodium	1.0	10	10.9	10	43.5	10	1.0
Specific conductance[5]	none	15	(17.0)	15	(39.0)	10	1.5
Sulfate	2.0	10	8.33	10	83.3	10	0.3
Turbidity[6]	none	5	none	none	none	none	none

[1]ANC: values in parentheses are in microequivalents per liter. For values within ±20 microequivalents per liter, an absolute DQO of ±6 microequivalents per liter is used for precision.

[2]Quality-control samples for organic monomeric aluminum are unavailable.

[3]Concentrations are expressed as micromoles carbon per liter.

[4]pH: percent error and coefficient of variation are calculated from $[H^+]$. Values in parentheses are in pH units.

[5]Specific conductance: values in parentheses are in microsiemens per centimeter.

[6]Comparison standards must be within 5 percent of the daily response factor of the instrument.

National Water Research Institute Ecosystem Interlaboratory QA Program

Interlaboratory-comparison graphs (fig. 4) are based on results from NWRI samples and represent NWRI studies from September 1999 through April 2001. Sample data with MCVs less than the Troy Laboratory reporting limits were excluded. The MCV and the control limits are represented by lines on the graphs; the percent difference (D) is calculated as:

$$D = \frac{AV - MCV}{MCV} \times 100 \tag{2}$$

where AV = analyzed value,

and MCV = mean concentration value.

A separate graph is shown for ANC values within the ±20-μeq/L range (fig. 4A2); these results are plotted as the difference between the laboratory value and the MCV. The pH results consist of two sets of data—values less than 6.00, and values equal to or greater than 6.00. The two sets of data have different DQOs, which are represented by a short dashed line and a long dashed line on the pH graph (fig. 4I).

Blind Reference Samples

Results from blind reference sample analyses are plotted in figure 5 by constituent and date of analysis. Sample data with MPVs less than the reporting limits were excluded. The MPV and the control limits of ±10 percent are represented by lines on the graphs; the percent difference (D) is calculated as:

$$D = \frac{AV - MPV}{MPV} \times 100 \tag{3}$$

where AV = analyzed value,

and MPV = most probable value.

Summary of Results

The following sections summarize the results for (A) QC samples (fig. 1), (B) filter blanks and analytical blanks (fig 2), (C) triplicate environmental samples (fig. 3), (D) SRS samples (table 3), (E) NWRI samples (fig. 4), and (F) blind samples (fig. 5).

A. Quality-Control Samples

Acid-Neutralizing Capacity (fig. 1A).—DQOs were met by 99 percent of the samples. The QC-high sample had a negative bias through July 2004 and a positive bias from December 2004 through June 2005. The QC-low sample had a positive bias in 2005.

Aluminum, Total Monomeric (fig. 1B).—DQOs were met by 99 percent of the samples. The QC samples had a positive bias from January 2004 through June 2005.

Aluminum, Organic Monomeric.—A QC sample has not been developed for this analysis. Separation-column efficiency is used to determine acceptability of the data.

Aluminum, Total (fig. 1C).—DQOs were met by 99 percent of the samples. The QC samples had a positive bias during this period.

Ammonium (fig. 1D).—DQOs were met by 99 percent of the samples. No apparent trends or biases were evident during this period.

Boron (fig. 1E).—DQOs were met by 100 percent of the samples. No apparent trends or biases were evident during this period.

Calcium (fig. 1F).—DQOs were met by 99 percent of the samples. No apparent trends or biases were evident for the QC-high sample; the QC-low sample had a negative bias during this period.

Carbon, Dissolved Organic (fig. 1G).—DQOs were met by 99 percent of the samples. The QC-high sample had a negative bias during this period. No apparent trends or biases were evident for the QC-low sample.

Chloride (fig. 1H).—DQOs were met by 99 percent of the samples. The QC-high sample had a positive bias during this period. No apparent trends or biases were evident for the QC-low sample.

Fluoride (fig. 1I).—DQOs were met by 98 percent of the samples. No apparent trends or biases were evident during this period.

Magnesium (fig. 1J).—DQOs were met by 100 percent of the samples. No apparent trends or biases were evident for the QC-high sample; the QC-low sample had a negative bias during this period.

Nitrate (ion chromatography) (fig. 1K).—DQOs were met by 99 percent of the samples. The QC-high sample had a positive bias during this period. No apparent trends or biases were evident for the QC-low sample.

Nitrate (colorimetric method) (fig. 1L).—DQOs were met by 88 percent of the samples. There are insufficient data to establish a trend for this period.

Nitrite (fig. 1M).—DQOs were met by 99 percent of the samples. The QC-high sample had a positive bias during this period. No apparent trends or biases were evident for the QC-low sample.

Nitrogen, Total Dissolved (fig. 1N).—DQOs were met by 99 percent of the samples. No apparent trends or biases were evident during this period.

pH (fig. 1O).—DQOs were met by 98 percent of the samples. No apparent trends or biases were evident for the QC-high sample; the QC-low sample had a positive bias in 2004 and 2005.

Potassium (fig. 1P).—DQOs were met by 100 percent of the samples. No apparent trends or biases were evident during this period.

Silicon (fig. 1Q).—DQOs were met by 99 percent of the samples. The QC-high sample had a positive bias during this period. The QC-low sample had a positive bias from October 2004 through June 2005.

Sodium (fig. 1R).—DQOs were met by 99 percent of the samples. The QC-high sample had a positive bias during this period. The QC-low sample had a positive bias in 2005.

Specific Conductance (fig. 1S).—DQOs were met by 100 percent of the samples. The QC samples had a negative bias during this period.

Sulfate (fig. 1T).—DQOs were met by 99 percent of the samples. The QC-high sample had a positive bias during this period. No apparent trends or biases were evident for the QC-low sample.

Turbidity.—Comparison standards are compared to the daily response factor of the instrument and used to determine acceptability of the data.

B. Filter Blanks and Analytical Blanks

Acid-Neutralizing Capacity.—Blanks were not analyzed for this constituent during this period.

Aluminum, Total Monomeric (fig. 2A).—The DQO was met by 99 percent of the samples. No systematic trends were evident for this analysis.

Aluminum, Organic Monomeric (fig. 2B).—The DQO was met by 99 percent of the samples. No systematic trends were evident for this analysis.

Aluminum, Total (fig. 2C).—The DQO was met for 84 percent of the samples. No systematic trends were evident for this analysis.

Ammonium (fig. 2D).—The DQO was met by 96 percent of the samples. No systematic trends were evident for this analysis.

Boron (fig. 2E).—The DQO was met by 100 percent of the samples. There are insufficient data to establish a trend for this period.

Calcium (fig. 2F).—The DQO was met by 92 percent of the samples. No systematic trends were evident for this analysis.

Carbon, Dissolved Organic (fig. 2G).—The DQO was not met for DOC. Blank data results are significantly higher in DOC concentrations since a new instrument was purchased in 1998. The current DQO is being evaluated and method modifications are being considered.

Chloride (fig. 2H).—The DQO was met by 94 percent of the samples. A long-term chloride contamination problem has continued to improve.

Fluoride (fig. 2I).—The DQO was met by 73 percent of the samples. No systematic trends were evident for this analysis.

Magnesium (fig. 2J).—The DQO was met by 97 percent of the samples. No systematic trends were evident for this analysis.

Nitrate (ion chromatography) (fig. 2K).—The DQO was met by 99 percent of the samples. No systematic trends were evident for this analysis.

Nitrate (colorimetric method).—Blanks were not available for this constituent during this period.

Nitrite (fig. 2L).—The DQO was met by 100 percent of the samples. No systematic trends were evident for this analysis.

Nitrogen, Total Dissolved (fig. 2M).—The DQO was met by 84 percent of the samples. No systematic trends were evident for this analysis.

pH.—Blanks were not analyzed for this constituent during this period.

Potassium (fig. 2N).—The DQO was met by 99 percent of the samples. Potassium analysis began on an inductively coupled plasma spectrophotometer in 2005; improved blank data are apparent.

Silicon (fig. 2O).—The DQO was met by 99 percent of the samples. No systematic trends were evident for this analysis.

Sodium (fig. 2P).—The DQO was met by 99 percent of the samples. Sodium analysis began on an inductively coupled plasma spectrophotometer in 2005; improved blank data are apparent.

Specific Conductance (fig. 2Q).—The DQO was met by 90 percent of the samples. No systematic trends were evident for this analysis.

Sulfate (fig. 2R).—The DQO was met by 98 percent of the samples. No systematic trends were evident for this analysis.

Turbidity.—Blanks were not analyzed for this constituent during this period.

C. Triplicate Environmental Samples

Acid-Neutralizing Capacity (figs. 3A1 and 3A2).—The DQO was met by 85 percent of the triplicate samples.

Aluminum, Total Monomeric (fig. 3B).—The DQO was met by 82 percent of the triplicate samples.

Aluminum, Organic Monomeric (fig. 3C).—The DQO was met by 91 percent of the triplicate samples.

Aluminum, Total (fig. 3D).—The DQO was met by 77 percent of the triplicate samples.

Ammonium (fig. 3E).—The DQO was not met for ammonium triplicate samples.

Boron.—Triplicate samples were not available for this constituent during this period.

Calcium (fig. 3F).—The DQO was met by 90 percent of the triplicate samples.

Carbon, Dissolved Organic (fig. 3G).—The DQO was met by 89 percent of the triplicate samples.

Chloride (fig. 3H).—The DQO was met by 80 percent of the triplicate samples.

Fluoride (fig. 3I).—The DQO was met by 76 percent of the triplicate samples.

Magnesium (fig. 3J).—The DQO was met by 95 percent of the triplicate samples.

Nitrate (ion chromatography) (fig. 3K).—The DQO was met by 79 percent of the triplicate samples.

Nitrate (colorimetric method).—Triplicate samples were not available for this constituent during this period.

Nitrite.—Triplicate samples were not available for this constituent during this period.

Nitrogen, Total Dissolved (fig. 3L).—The DQO was not met for total dissolved nitrogen triplicate samples.

pH (fig. 3M).—The DQO was met by 99 percent of the triplicate samples.

Potassium (fig. 3N).—The DQO was met by 94 percent of the triplicate samples.

Silicon (fig. 3O).—The DQO was met by 99 percent of the triplicate samples.

Sodium (fig. 3P).—The DQO was met by 95 percent of the triplicate samples.

Specific Conductance (fig. 3Q).—The DQO was met by 99 percent of the triplicate samples.

Sulfate (fig. 3R).—The DQO was met by 99 percent of the triplicate samples.

Turbidity.—Triplicate samples were not available for this constituent during this period.

D. U.S. Geological Survey's Standard Reference Sample Project

The USGS SRS project rates laboratory performance for each analyte on a scale of 4 to 0. Beginning with the spring 2005 study, the SRS project discontinued the use of laboratory ratings and instead reports a percent difference from the MPV for each analyte. The Troy laboratory DQO is ±10 percent from the MPV.

Rating	Performance
4.0	Excellent
3.0–3.99	Good
2.0–2.99	Satisfactory
1.0–1.99	Marginal
0.0–0.99	Unsatisfactory

Overall laboratory mean ratings for each SRS sample were (sample no., rating):

T–175	3.0	N–79	2.5	P–41	2.8
T–177	3.6	N–81	2.5	P–42	3.3
T–179	3.0	N–83	2.0	P–43	3.3

Missing SRS results for the Troy Laboratory were due to instrument downtime during the SRS study period.

All analyses (table 3) received a satisfactory or better rating for each constituent with these exceptions:

Aluminum.—The cause of a zero ratings for SRS T–175 and T–179 and the 28.8 percent high value for T–181 is unknown and being investigated.

Chloride.—The zero and marginal ratings for SRS P–41 and P–43 were for values which were within 12 percent and 10 percent of the SRS MPVs, respectively. The cause of the zero rating for P–42 is erroneous data entry.

Nitrate.—The marginal rating for SRS N–81 was for a value which was 10 percent above the SRS most probable value.

E. National Water Research Institute Ecosystem Interlaboratory QA Program

Environment Canada's NWRI program does not audit the Troy Laboratory analysis of total monomeric aluminum, organic monomeric aluminum, boron, fluoride, nitrate (colorimetric method), nitrite, total dissolved nitrogen, and turbidity.

Acid-Neutralizing Capacity (figs. 4A1 and 4A2).—The DQO was met by 55 percent of the NWRI samples. The cause of the inconsistent results is unknown. Data were not submitted for study 84 due to instrument downtime.

Aluminum, Total (fig. 4B).—The DQO was met by 77 percent of the NWRI samples. The cause of the high outliers is unknown.

13

Table 3. Results obtained by the USGS Laboratory in Troy, N.Y., for the U.S. Geological Survey Standard Reference Sample (SRS) Project, fall 2003 through spring 2005.

[MPV, most probable value; TV, Troy Laboratory value. All values are in milligrams per liter except aluminum (micrograms per liter, µg/L), pH (pH units), and specific conductance (microsiemens per centimeter, µS/cm). Dashes indicate no results reported]

Analyte	MPV, TV, and rating[a]	SRS sample number and date of sample distribution											
		T-175 Fall 03[b]	N-79 Fall 03[b]	P-41 Fall 03[b]	T-177 Spring 04[b]	N-81 Spring 04[b]	P-42 Spring 04[b]	T-179 Fall 04[b]	N-83 Fall 04[b]	P-43 Fall 04[b]	T-181 Spring 05[b]	N-85 Spring 05[b]	P-44 Spring 05[b]
Aluminum	MPV	52	—	—	76.5	—	—	51.7	—	—	16.2	—	—
	TV	78.1	—	—	79	—	—	62.3	—	—	20.9	—	—
	Rating	0	—	—	4	—	—	0	—	—	(28.80)[e]	—	—
Ammonium[c]	MPV	—	0.1	—	—	0.18	—	—	—	—	—	—	—
	TV	—	0.11	—	—	0.18	—	—	—	—	—	—	—
	Rating	—	2	—	—	4	—	—	—	—	—	—	—
Boron	MPV	48.3	—	—	90.7	—	—	—	—	—	—	—	—
	TV	48.3	—	—	92	—	—	—	—	—	—	—	—
	Rating	4	—	—	4	—	—	—	—	—	—	—	—
Calcium	MPV	8.76	—	0.55	31.4	—	0.495	18.9	—	0.53	13.4	—	0.52
	TV	9.1	—	0.567	32.3	—	0.502	18.8	—	0.518	13.5	—	0.502
	Rating	3	—	3	3	—	4	4	—	4	(0.86)[e]	—	(-3.46)[e]
Chloride	MPV	—	—	5.88	—	—	6.12	—	—	4.9	—	—	2.33
	TV	—	—	5.17	—	—	3.14	—	—	4.41	—	—	2.51
	Rating	—	—	0	—	—	0	—	—	1	—	—	(7.51)[e]
Magnesium	MPV	2.03	—	0.054	7.63	—	0.048	4.59	—	0.042	3.05	—	0.094
	TV	2.04	—	0.047	7.76	—	0.046	4.64	—	0.039	3.08	—	0.085
	Rating	4	—	2	4	—	3	4	—	4	(0.89)[e]	—	(-9.57)[e]
Nitrate	MPV	—	0.13	—	—	0.182	—	—	0.066	—	—	0.175	—
	TV	—	0.14	—	—	0.2	—	—	0.06	—	—	0.184	—
	Rating	—	3	—	—	1	—	—	2	—	—	(4.86)[e]	—
pH	MPV	—	—	3.94	—	—	3.9	—	—	3.99	—	—	—
	TV	—	—	3.94	—	—	3.96	—	—	4.05	—	—	—
	Rating	—	—	4	—	—	4	—	—	4	—	—	—

Table 3. Results obtained by the USGS Laboratory in Troy, N.Y., for the U.S. Geological Survey Standard Reference Sample (SRS) Project, fall 2003 through spring 2005 - Continued.

[MPV, most probable value; TV, Troy Laboratory value. All values are in milligrams per liter except aluminum (micrograms per liter, µg/L), pH (pH units), and specific conductance (microsiemens per centimeter, µS/cm). Dashes indicate no results reported]

| Analyte | MPV, TV, and rating[a] | SRS sample number and date of sample distribution | | | | | | | | | | | |
		T-175 Fall 03[b]	N-79 Fall 03[b]	P-41 Fall 03[b]	T-177 Spring 04[b]	N-81 Spring 04[b]	P-42 Spring 04[b]	T-179 Fall 04[b]	N-83 Fall 04[b]	P-43 Fall 04[b]	T-181 Spring 05[b]	N-85 Spring 05[b]	P-44 Spring 05[b]
Potassium	MPV	3.83	—	0.072	3.3	—	0.325	—	—	—	—	—	—
	TV	3.95	—	0.09	3.17	—	0.325	—	—	—	—	—	—
	Rating	3	—	2	3	—	4	—	—	—	—	—	—
Silicon[d]	MPV	5.6	—	—	10.6	—	—	14.9	—	—	13.1	—	—
	TV	5.73	—	—	10.9	—	—	15.1	—	—	13.6	—	—
	Rating	4	—	—	3	—	—	4	—	—	(3.82)[e]	—	—
Sodium	MPV	8.63	—	—	37.2	—	0.304	—	—	—	—	—	—
	TV	8.35	—	—	37.7	—	0.3	—	—	—	—	—	—
	Rating	3	—	—	4	—	4	—	—	—	—	—	—
Specific conductance	MPV	—	—	58.7	—	—	63.2	—	—	51.7	—	—	—
	TV	—	—	58.7	—	—	60.4	—	—	48.9	—	—	—
	Rating	—	—	4	—	—	3	—	—	3	—	—	—
Sulfate	MPV	—	—	0.32	—	—	0.344	—	—	0.536	—	—	1.14
	TV	—	—	0.26	—	—	0.3	—	—	0.424	—	—	1.15
	Rating	—	—	4	—	—	4	—	—	4	—	—	(0.91)[e]

[a]Laboratory rating system: 4 is highest score; 0 is lowest.
[b]Sample described at http://qadata.cr.usgs.gov/srs_study/reports/index.php.
[c]The SRS project reports data as "Ammonia as Nitrogen."
[d]The SRS project reports data as "Silica."
[e]Laboratory rating system change: values in parentheses are percent difference

15

Ammonium (fig. 4C).—The DQO was not met for the NWRI samples. The cause of the positive bias is currently being investigated. The reporting limit for ammonium is being reevaluated. Data were not submitted for studies 83 and 86 due to instrument downtime.

Calcium (fig. 4D).—The DQO was met by 88 percent of the NWRI samples. The data exhibited a positive bias during this period.

Carbon, Dissolved Organic (fig. 4E).—The DQO was met by 84 percent of the NWRI samples. The data exhibited a positive bias for this period.

Chloride (fig. 4F).—The DQO was met by 88 percent of the NWRI samples. The data exhibited a negative bias during this period.

Magnesium (fig. 4G).—The DQO was met by 100 percent of the NWRI samples. The data exhibited a negative bias during studies 84 and 86.

Nitrate (ion chromatography) (fig. 4H).—The DQO was met by 94 percent of the NWRI samples. The data exhibited a negative bias during study 83.

pH (fig. 4I).—The DQO was met by 100 percent of the NWRI samples. No trend or bias was evident. Data were not submitted for study 84 due to instrument downtime.

Potassium (fig. 4J).—The DQO was met by 94 percent of the NWRI samples. The data exhibited a negative bias during this period. Data were not submitted for studies 84 and 85 due to instrument upgrades.

Silicon (fig. 4K).—The DQO was met by 100 percent of the NWRI samples. The data exhibited a negative bias during this period.

Sodium (fig. 4L).—The DQO was met by 85 percent of the NWRI samples. The cause of the erratically low outliers is unknown. The data exhibited a positive bias during this period. Data was not submitted for studies 84 and 85 due to instrument upgrades.

Specific Conductance (fig. 4M).—The DQO was met by 100 percent of the NWRI samples. The data exhibited a negative bias during this period. Data were not submitted for study 84 due to instrument downtime.

Sulfate (fig. 4N).—The DQO was met by 100 percent of the NWRI samples. No trend or bias was evident.

F. Blind Reference Samples

Blind reference samples (SRS low-ionic-strength constituent P-samples) are analyzed for the Troy Laboratory procedures for which the SRS project reports an analyte MPV. The blind reference samples are not analyzed for acid-neutralizing capacity, total monomeric aluminum, organic monomeric aluminum, total aluminum, ammonium, boron, dissolved organic carbon, nitrate, nitrite, total dissolved nitrogen, silicon and turbidity.

Calcium (fig. 5A).—The DQO for calcium was met by 100 percent of the blind reference samples. The data exhibited a negative bias for this period.

Chloride (fig. 5B).—The DQO was met by 86 percent of the blind reference samples. A positive bias was evident through July 2004.

Fluoride (fig. 5C).—The DQO was not met for the fluoride blind reference samples. The data are being investigated.

Magnesium (fig. 5D).—The DQO was met by 86 percent of the blind reference samples. Most data indicated a negative bias.

pH (fig. 5E).—The DQO was met by 99 percent of the blind reference samples. A positive bias was evident during this period.

Potassium (fig. 5F).—The DQO was met by 96 percent of the blind reference samples. A negative bias was evident during this period.

Sodium (fig. 5G).—The DQO was met by 99 percent of the blind reference samples. No trend or bias was evident.

Specific Conductance (fig. 5H).—The DQO was met by 89 percent of the blind reference samples. A negative bias was evident during this period.

Sulfate (fig. 5I).—The DQO was met by 89 percent of the samples. No trend or bias was evident.

Selected References

Lawrence, G.B., Lincoln, T.A., Horan-Ross, D.A., Olson, M.L., and Waldron, L.A., 1995, Analytical methods of the U.S. Geological Survey's New York District Water Analysis Laboratory: U.S. Geological Survey Open-File Report 95–416, 78 p.

Lincoln, T.A., Horan-Ross, D.A., McHale, M.R., and Lawrence, G.B., 2001, Quality-assurance data for routine water analyses by the U.S. Geological Survey Laboratory in Troy, New York—July 1993 through June 1995: U.S. Geological Survey Open-File Report 01–171, 25 p.

Lincoln, T.A., Horan-Ross, D.A., McHale, M.R., and Lawrence, G.B., 2004, Quality-assurance data for routine water analyses by the U.S. Geological Survey Laboratory in Troy, New York—July 1995 through June 1997: U.S. Geological Survey Open-File Report 2004–1327, 25 p.

Lincoln, T.A., Horan-Ross, D.A., McHale, M.R., and Lawrence, G.B., 2006, Quality-assurance data for routine water analyses by the U.S. Geological Survey Laboratory in Troy, New York—July 1997 through June 1999: U.S. Geological Survey Open-File Report 2006–1245, 25 p.

Lincoln, T.A., Horan-Ross, D.A., McHale, M.R., and Lawrence, G.B., 2006, Quality-assurance data for routine water analyses by the U.S. Geological Survey Laboratory in Troy, New York—July 1999 through June 2001: U.S. Geological Survey Open-File Report 2006–1246, 27 p.

Lincoln, T.A., Horan-Ross, D.A., McHale, M.R., and Lawrence, G.B., 2009, Quality-assurance data for routine water analyses by the U.S. Geological Survey Laboratory in Troy, New York—July 2001 through June 2003: U.S. Geological Survey Open-File Report 2009–1232, 32 p.

Lincoln, T.A., Horan-Ross, D.A., Olson, M.L., and Lawrence, G.B., 1996, Quality-assurance data for routine water analyses by the U.S. Geological Survey Laboratory in Troy, New York—May 1991 through June 1993: U.S. Geological Survey Open-File Report 96–167, 22 p.

This page has been left blank intentionally.

Figures 1-5

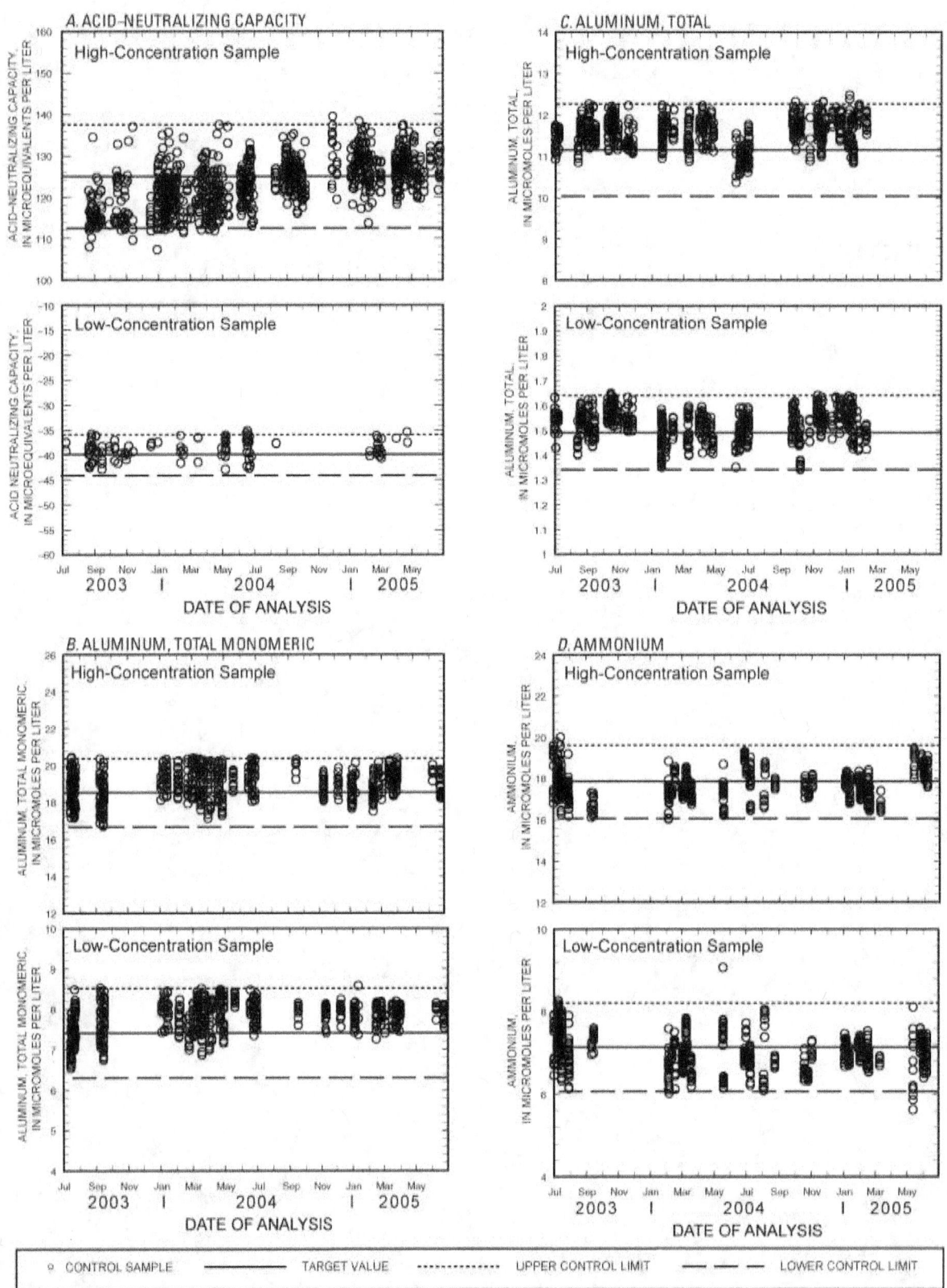

Figure 1. High- and low-concentration quality-control sample results: A. Acid-neutralizing capacity. B. Aluminum, total monomeric. C. Aluminum, total. D. Ammonium.

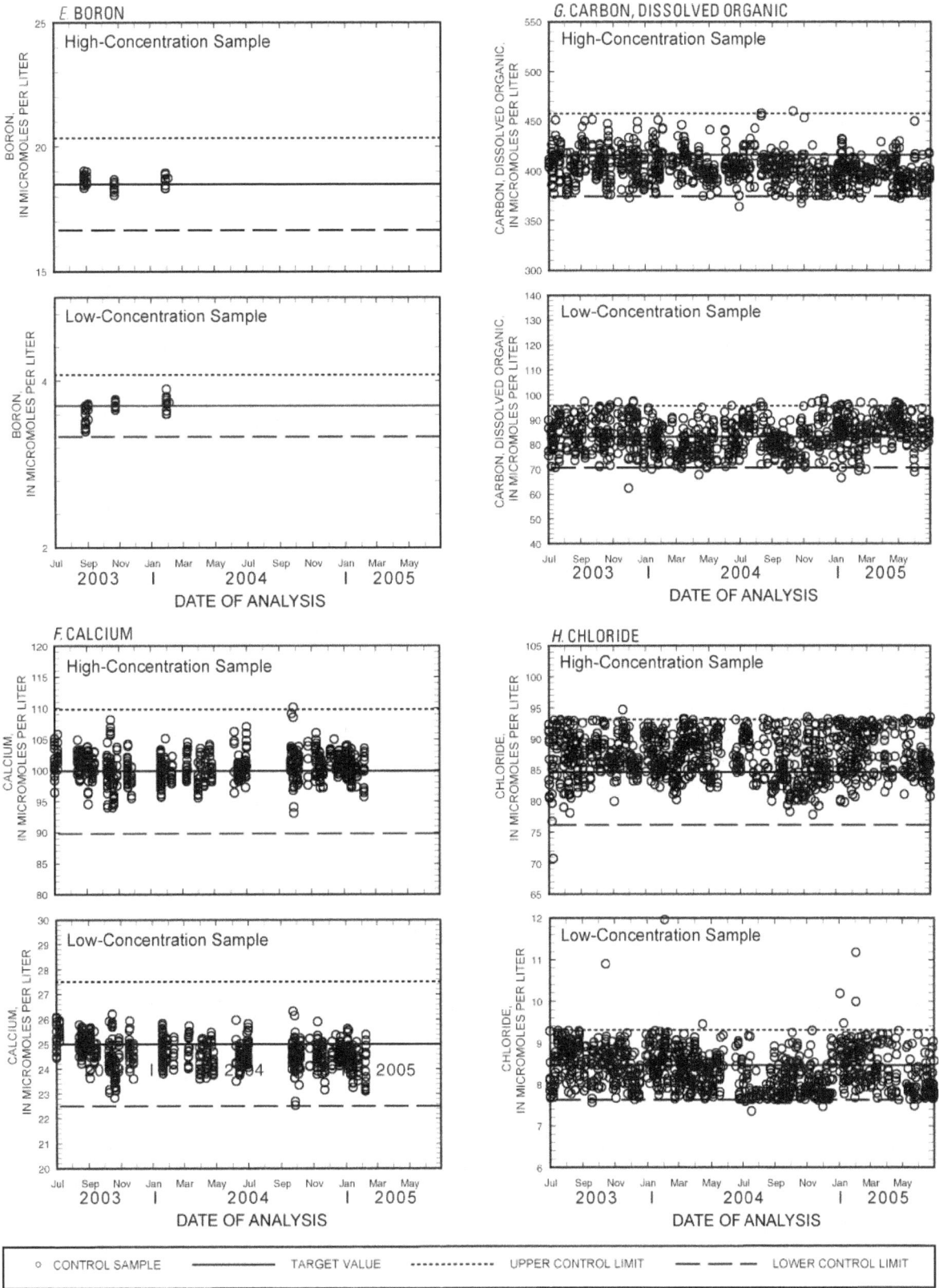

Figure 1. High- and low-concentration quality-control sample results (continued): *E.* Boron. *F.* Calcium *G.*Carbon, dissolved organic. *H.* Chloride.

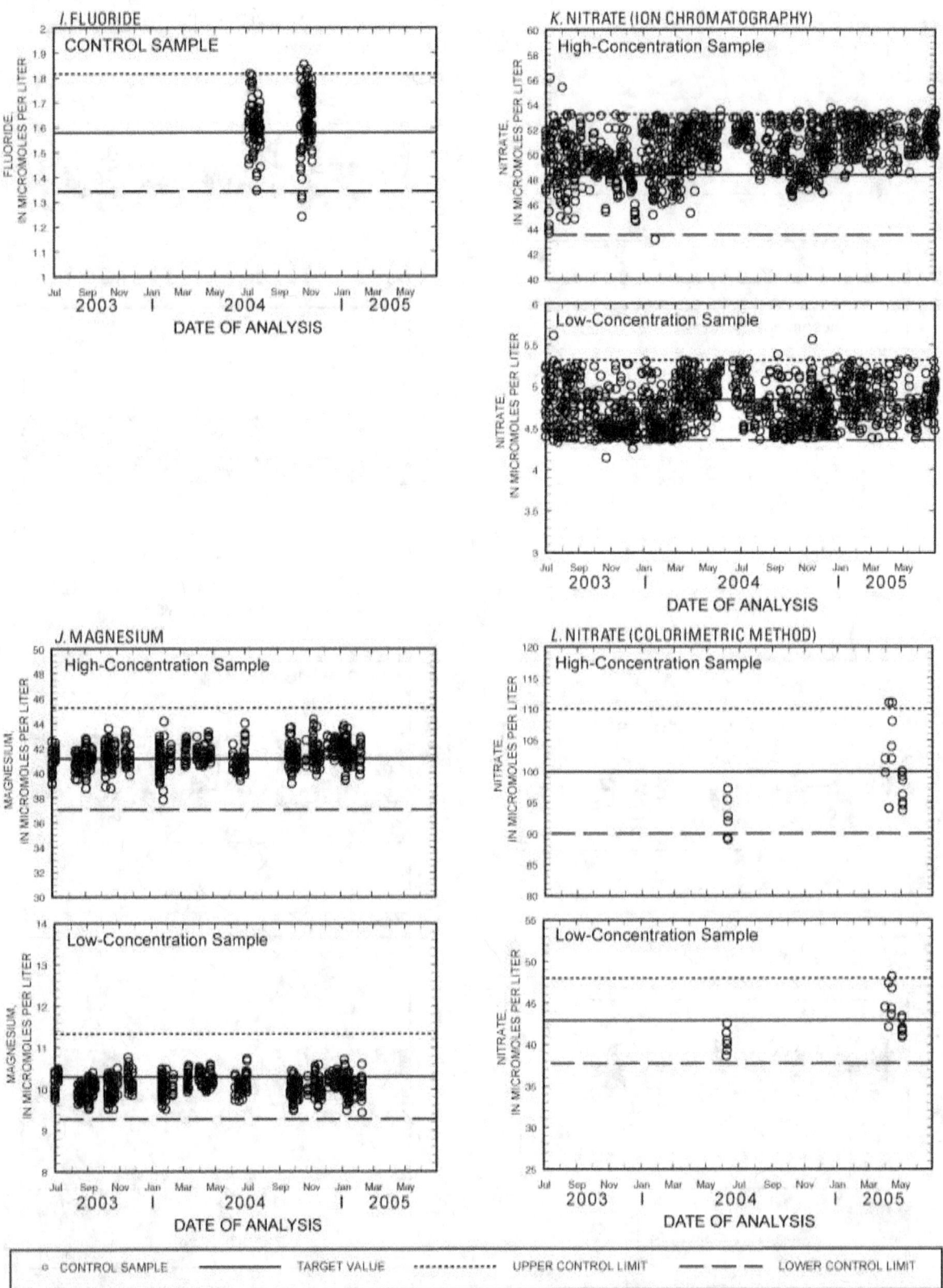

Figure 1. High- and low-concentration quality-control sample results (continued): *I*. Fluoride. *J*. Magnesium. *K*. Nitrate (ion chromatography). *L*. Nitrate (colorimetric method).

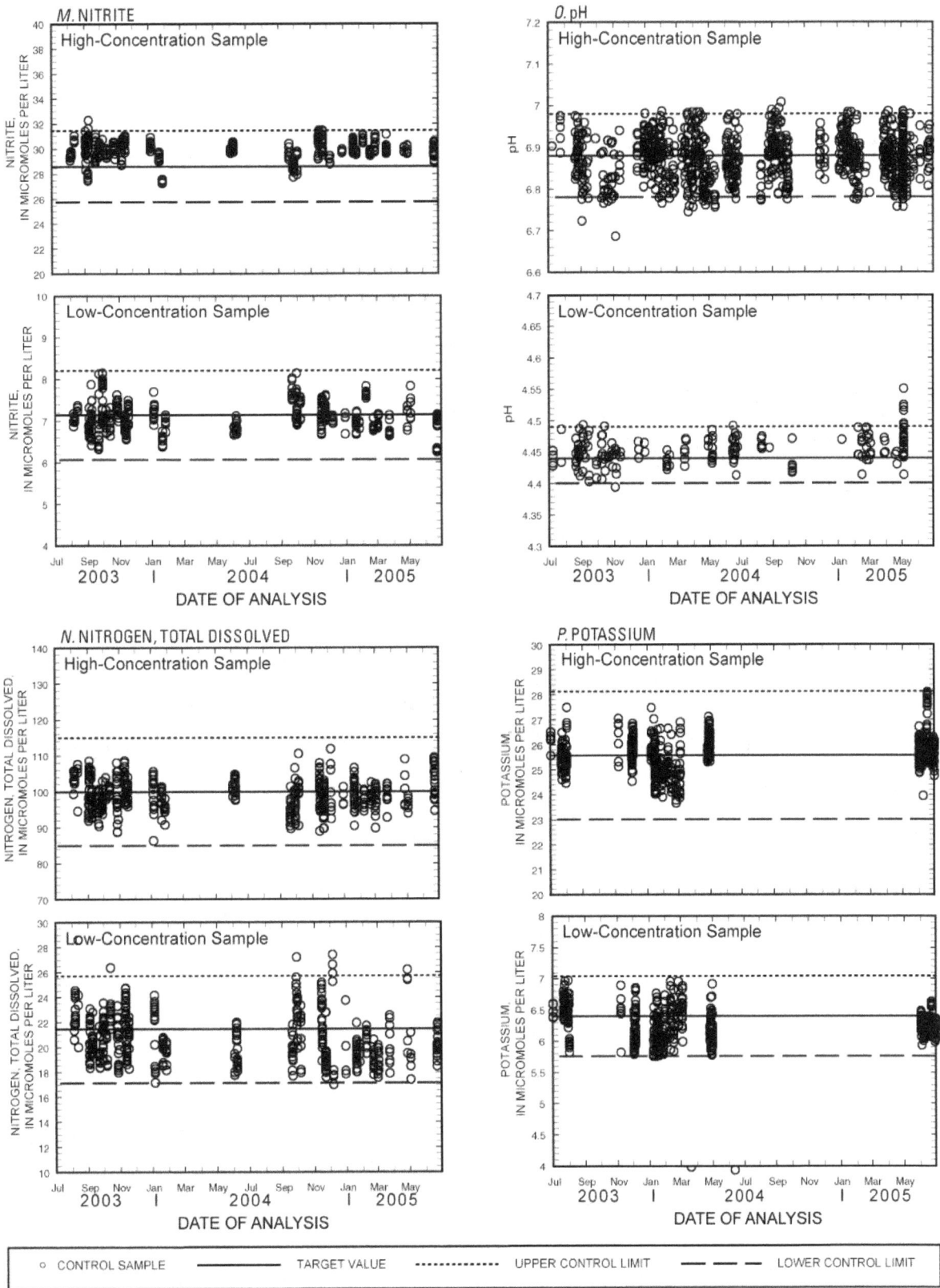

Figure 1. High- and low-concentration quality-control sample results (continued): *M.* Nitrate. *N.* Nitrogen, total dissolved. *O.* pH. *P.* Potassium.

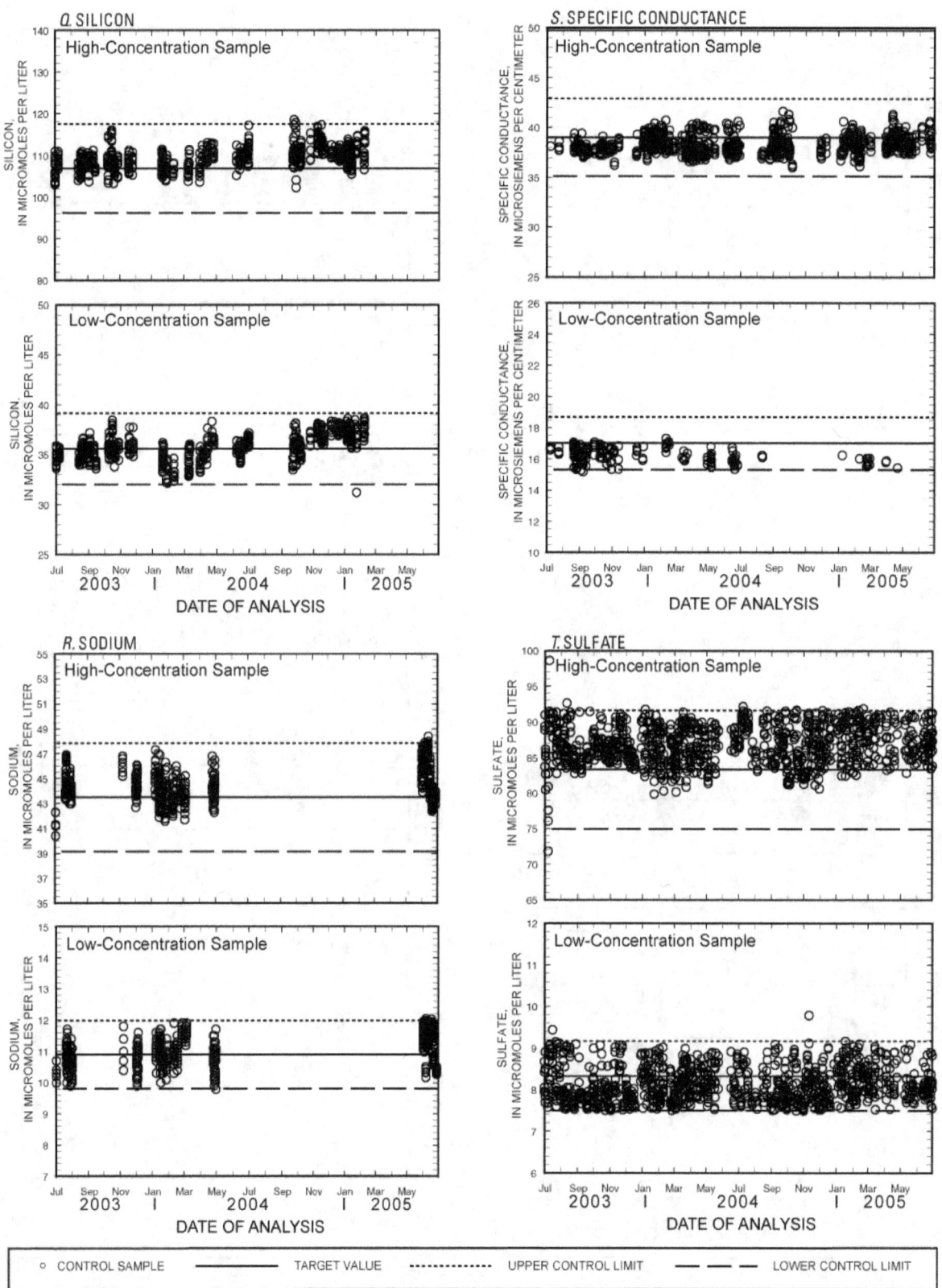

Figure 1. High- and low-concentration quality-control sample results (continued): *Q.* Silicon. *R.* Sodium. *S.* Specific Conductance. *T.* Sulfate.

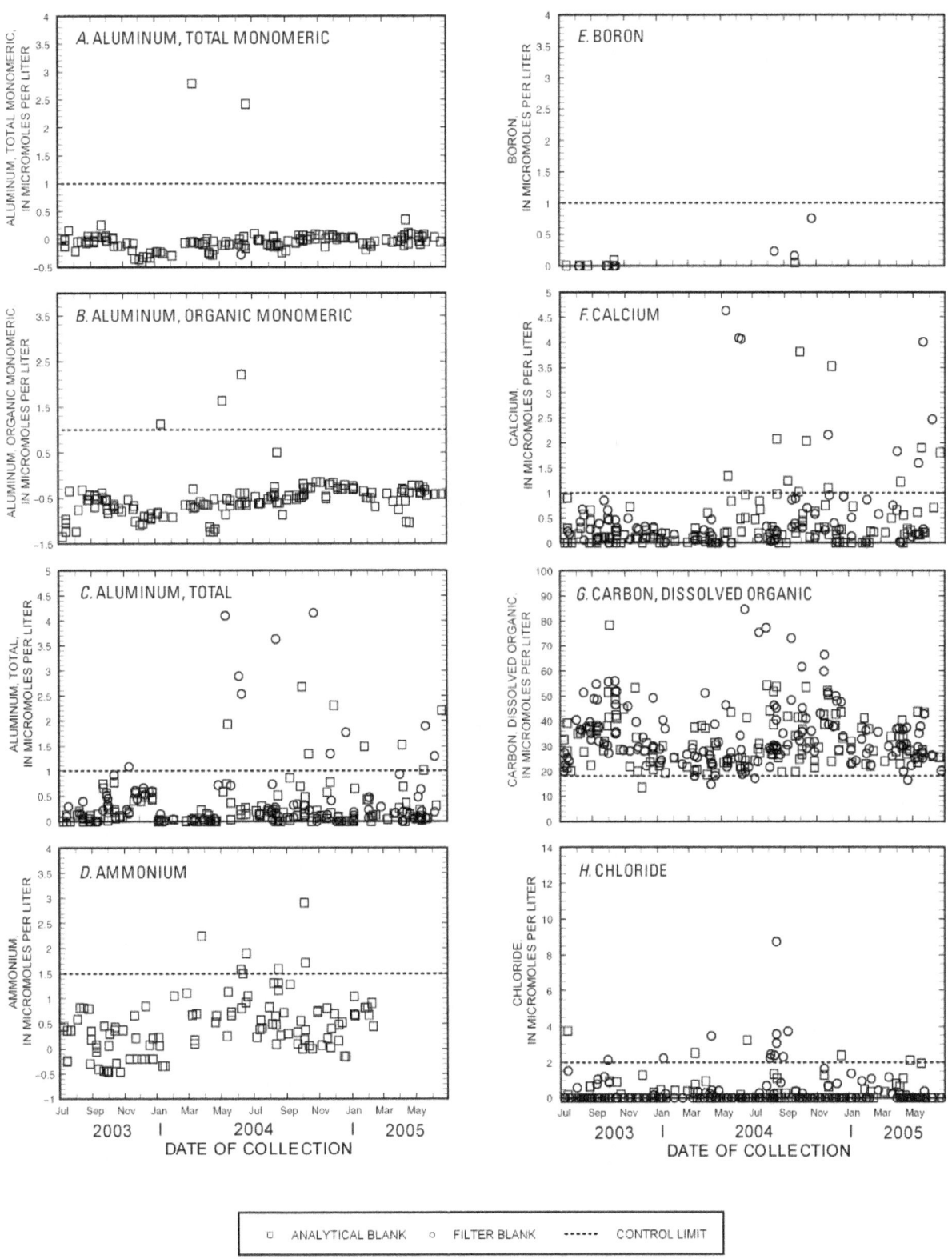

Figure 2. Filter-blank and analytical-blank sample results: *A.* Aluminum, total monomeric. *B.* Aluminum, organic monomeric. *C.* Aluminum, total. *D.* Ammonium. *E.* Boron. *F.* Calcium. *G.* Carbon, dissolved organic. *H.* Chloride.

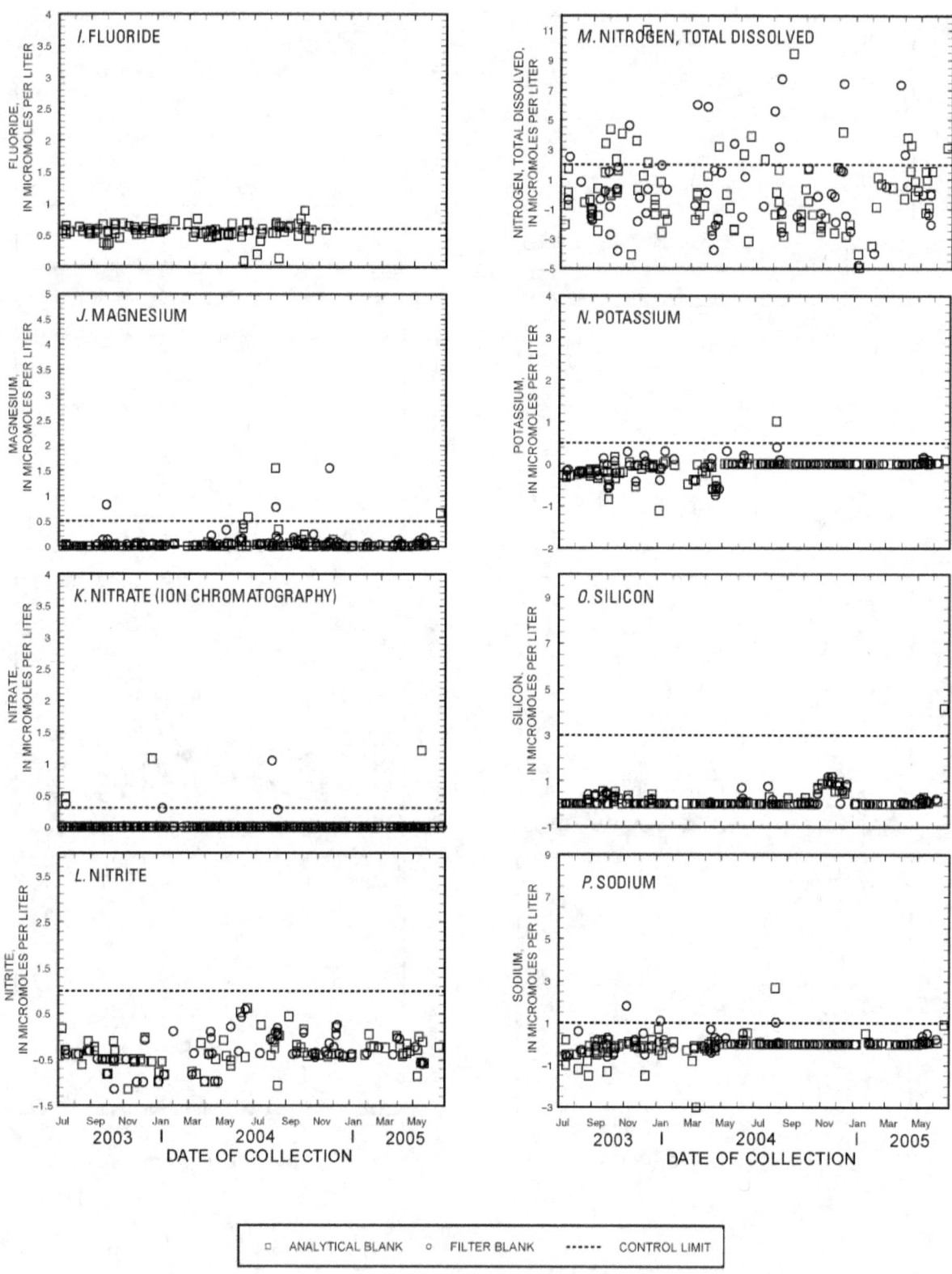

Figure 2. Filter-blank and analytical-blank sample results (continued): *I.* Fluoride. *J.* Magnesium. *K.* Nitrate (ion chromatography). *L.* Nitrate. *M.* Nitrogen, total dissolved. *N.* Potassium. *O.* Silicon. *P.* Sodium.

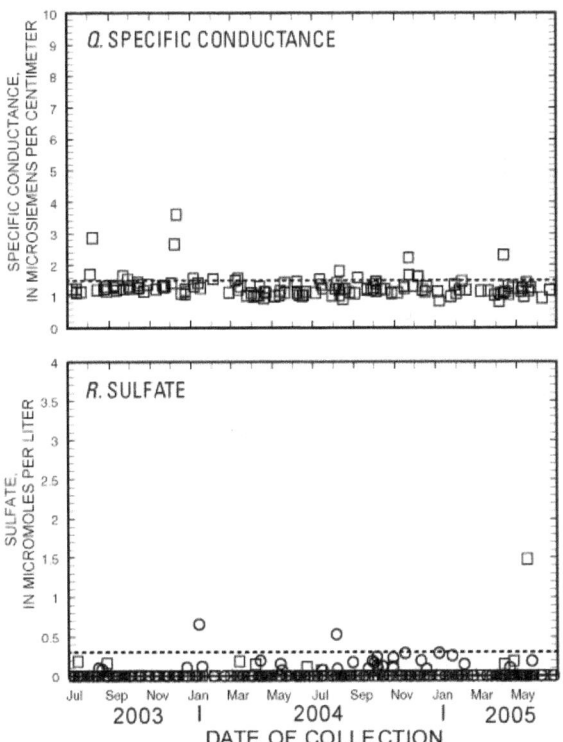

Figure 2. Filter-blank and analytical-blank sample results (continued): *Q.* Specific conductance. *R.* Sulfate.

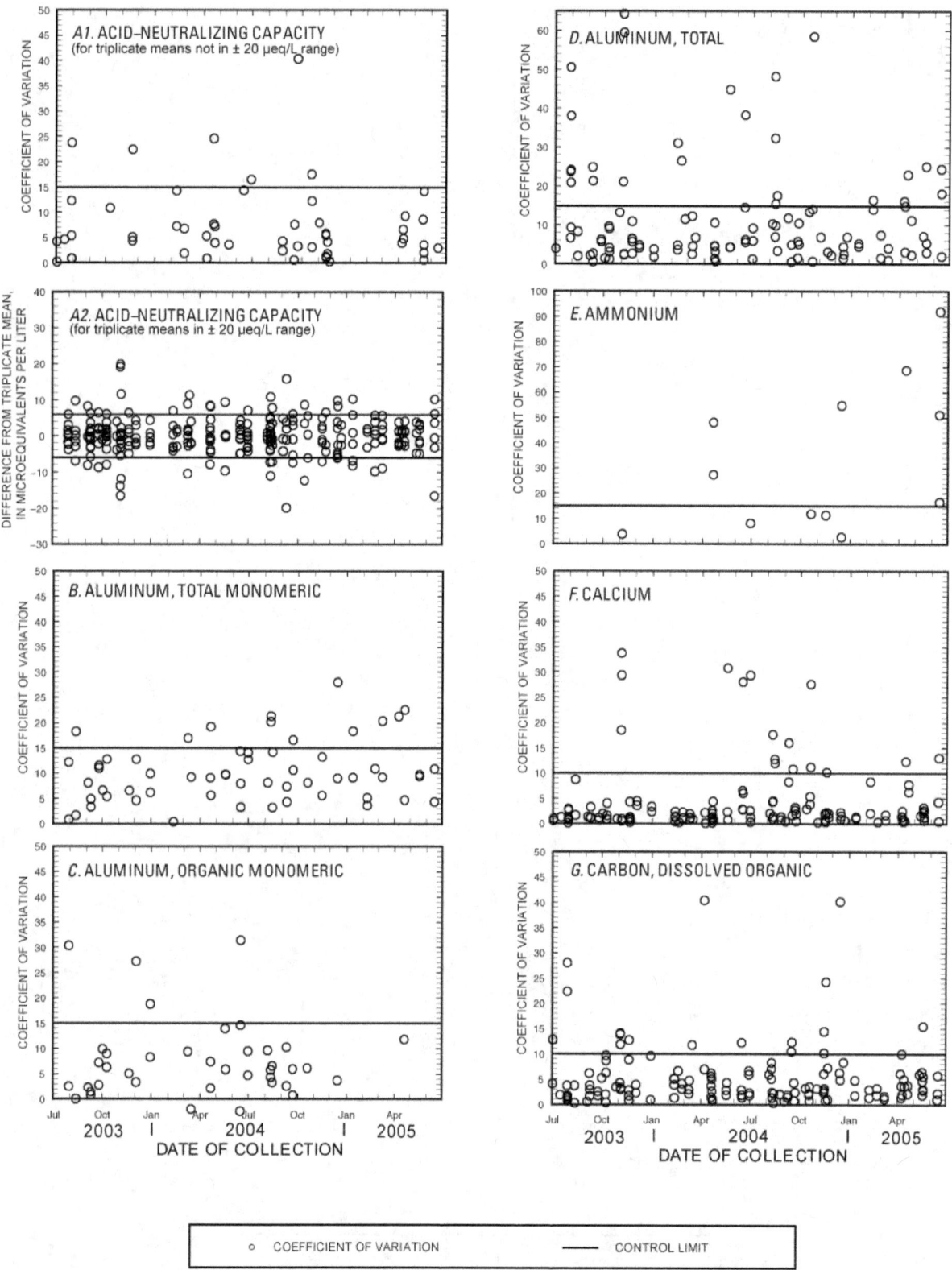

Figure 3. Triplicate environmental samples: *A1.* Acid-neutralizing capacity (for triplicate means not in ±20μeq/L range). *A2.* Acid-neutralizing capacity (for triplicate means not in ±20μeq/L range). *B.* Aluminum, total monomeric. *C.* Aluminum, organic monomeric. *D.* Aluminum, total. *E.* Ammonium. *F.* Calcium. *G.* Carbon, dissolved organic.

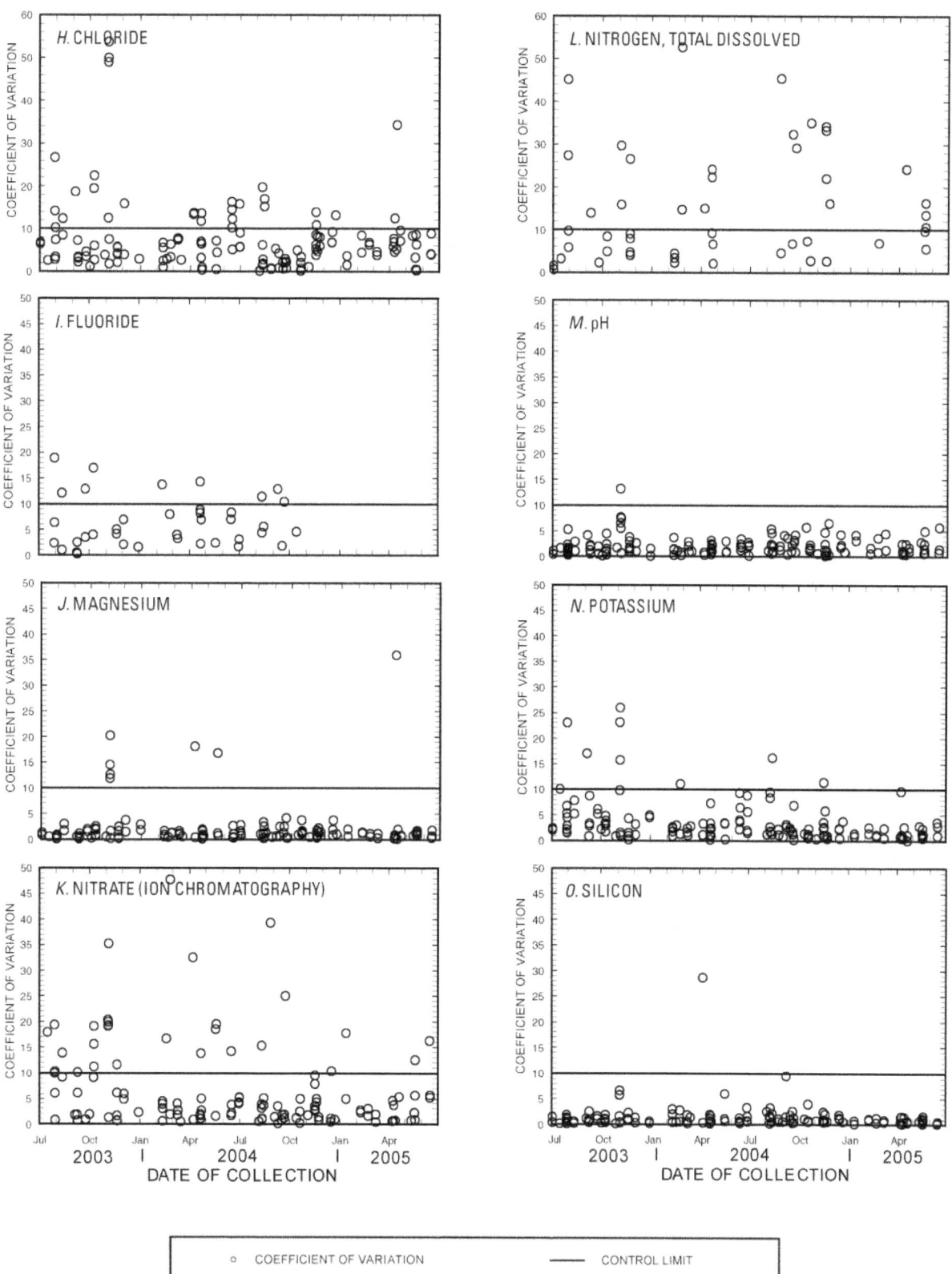

Figure 3. Triplicate environmental sample results (continued): *H.* Chloride. *I.* Fluoride. *J.* Magnesium. *K.* Nitrate (ion chromatography). *L.* Nitrogen, total dissolved. *M.* pH. *N.* Potassium. *O.* Silicon.

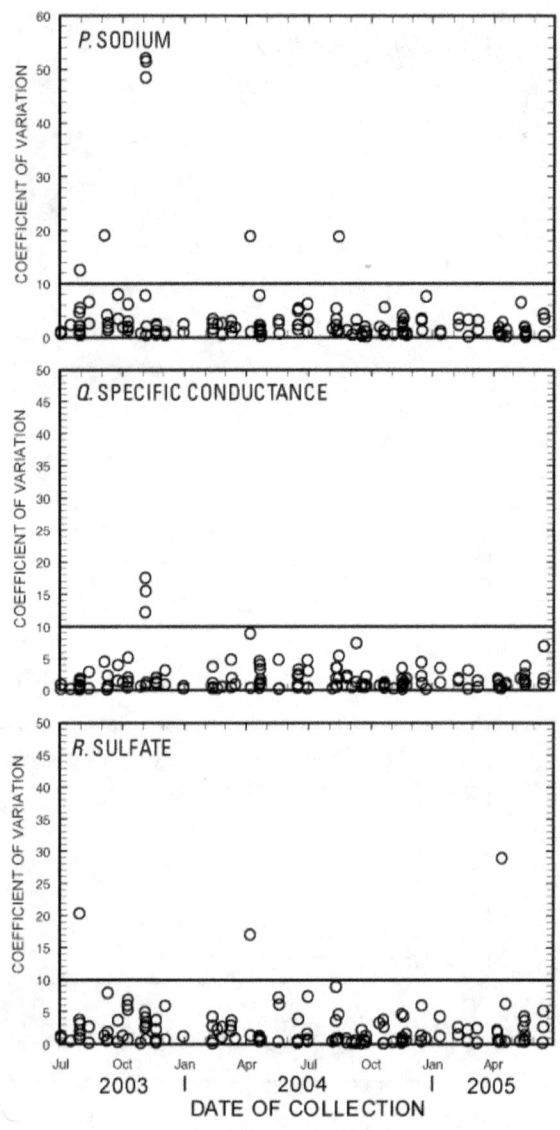

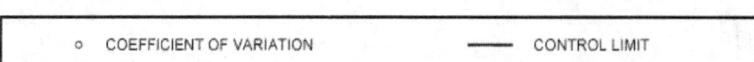

Figure 3. Triplicate environmental sample results (continued): *P.* Sodium. *Q.* Specific Conductance. *R.* Sulfate.

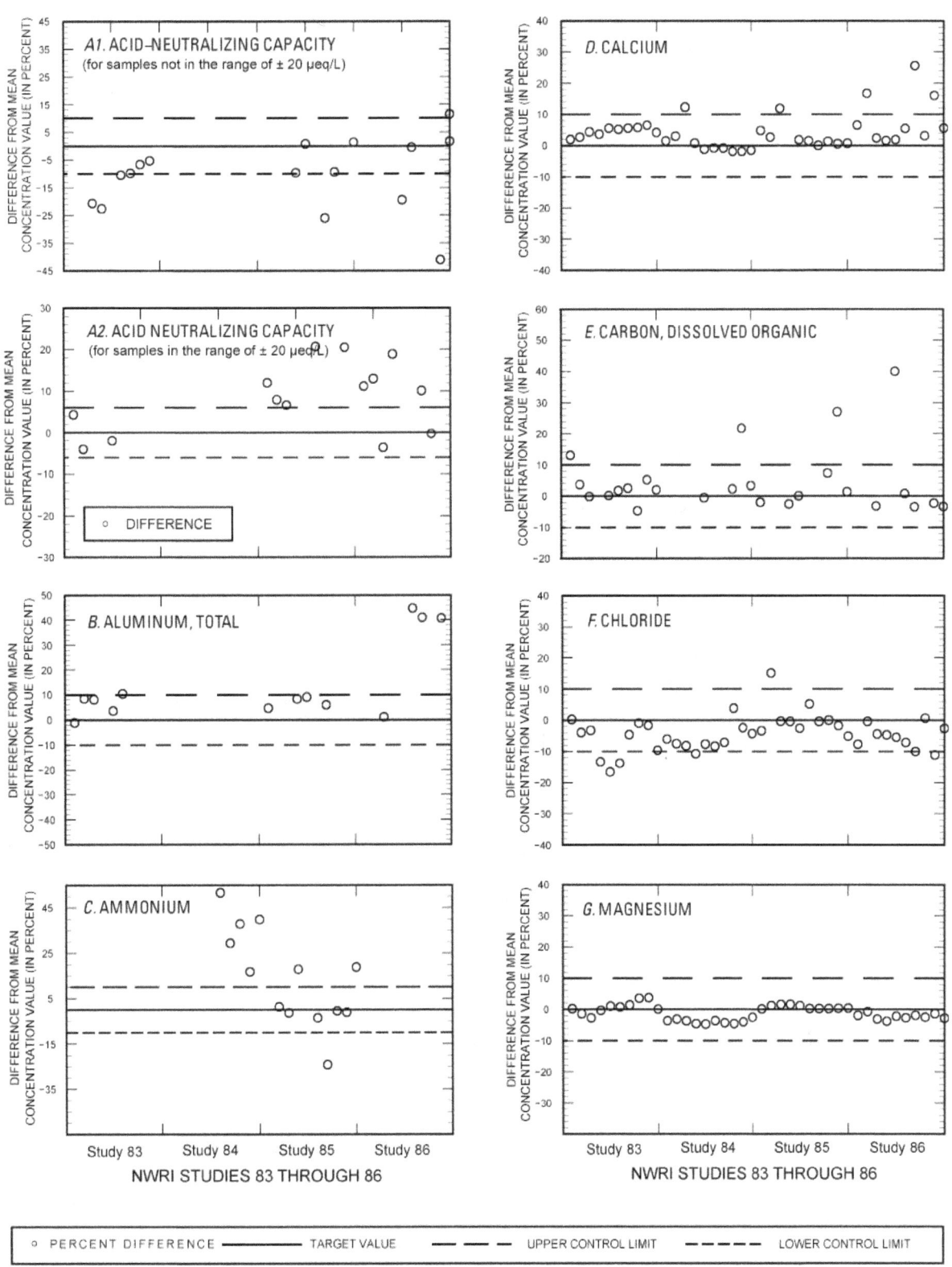

Figure 4. NWRI Ecosystem Interlaboratory QA Program results: *A1.* Acid-neutralizing capacity (for means not in the range of ± 20µeq/L). *A2.* Acid-neutralizing capacity (for means in the range of ± 20µeq/L). *B.* Aluminum, total. *C.* Ammonium. *D.* Calcium. *E.* Carbon, dissolved organic. *F.* Chloride. *G.* Magnesium.

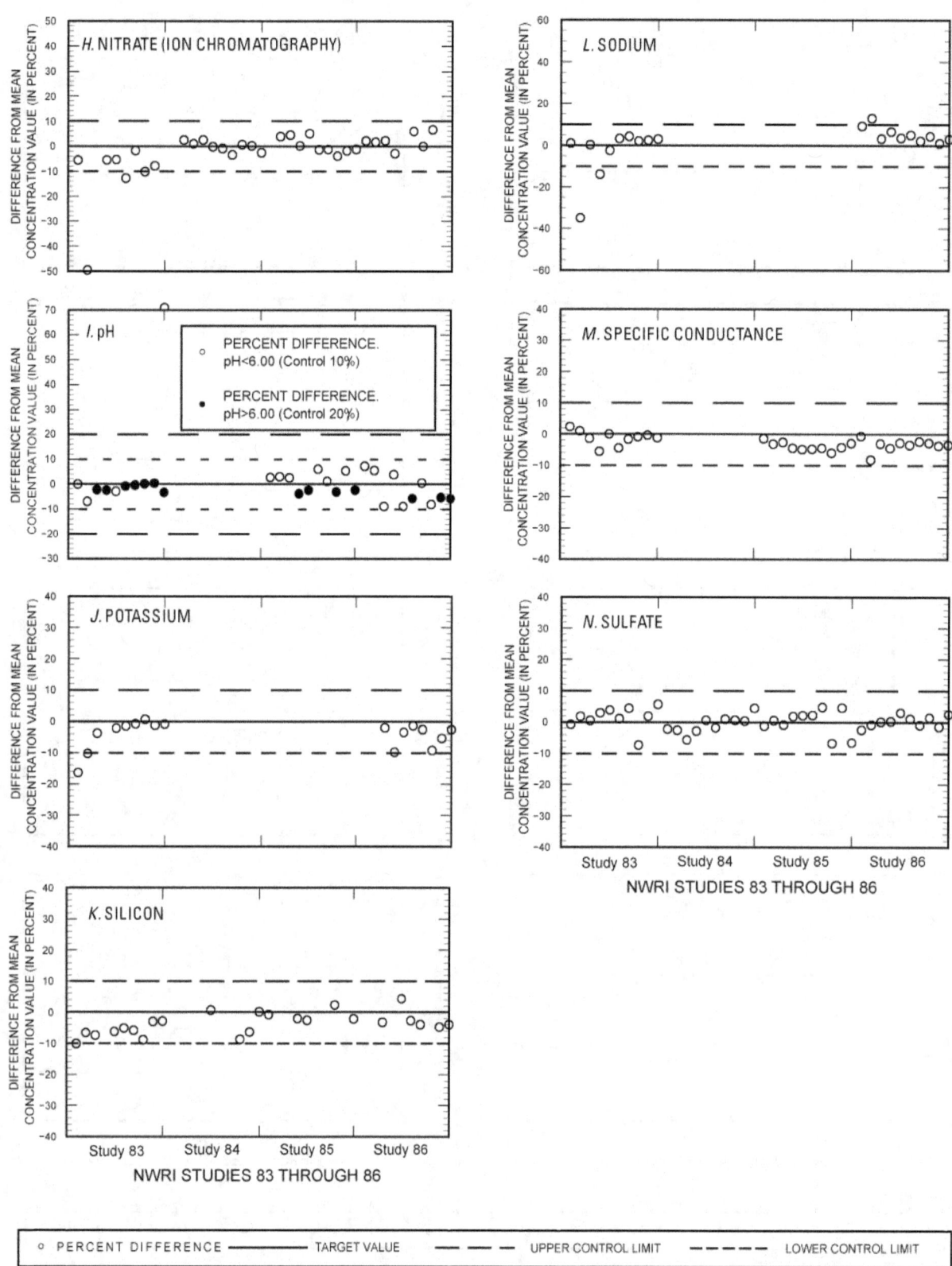

Figure 4. NWRI Ecosystem Interlaboratory QA Program results (continued): *H.* Nitrate (ion chromotography). *I.* pH. *J.* Potassium. *K.* Silicon. *L.* Sodium. *M.* Specific conductance. *N.* Sulfate.

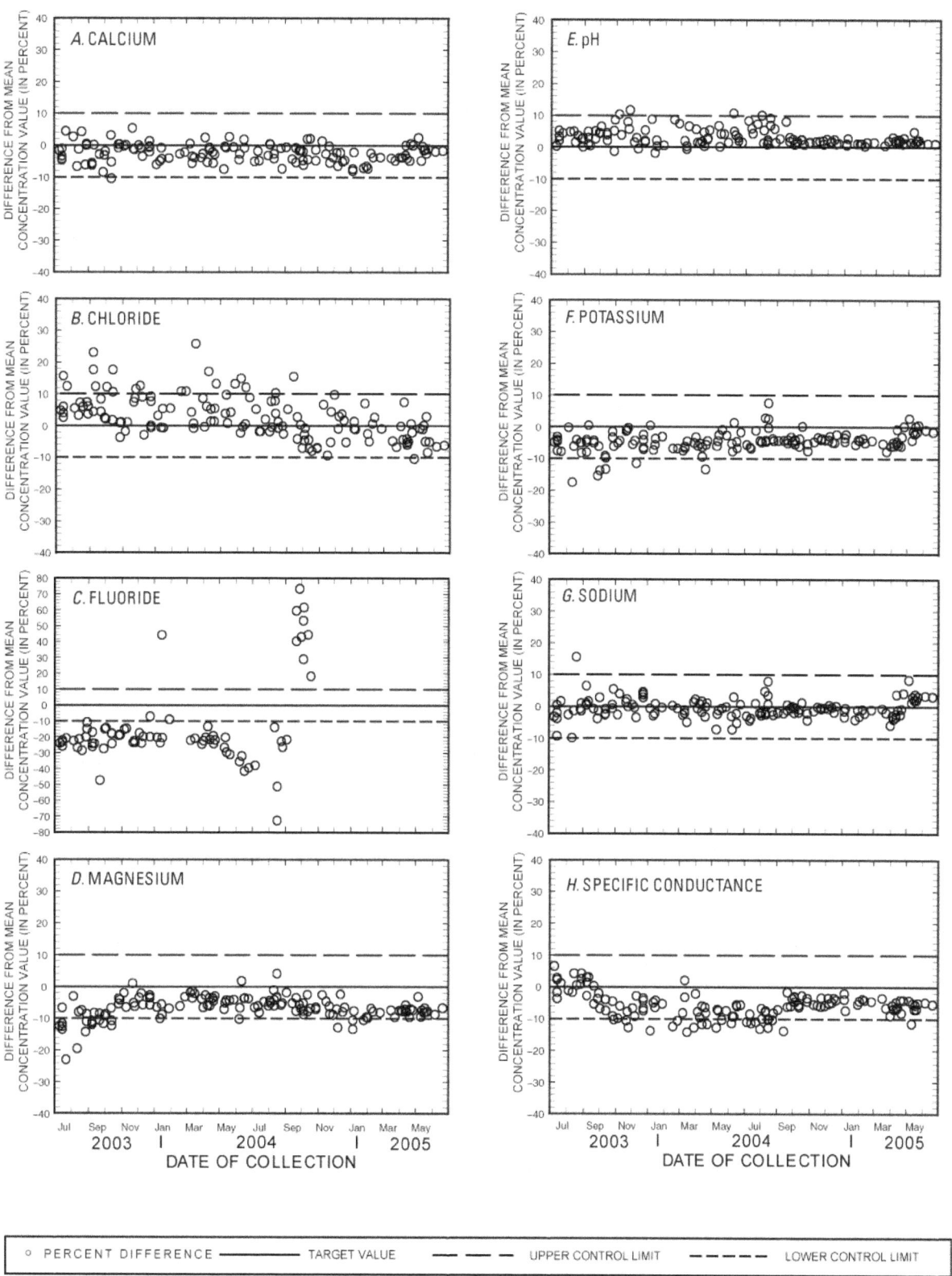

Figure 5. Blind reference sample results: *A.* Calcium. *B.* Chloride. *C.* Fluoride. *D.* Magnesium. *E.* pH.
F. Potassium. *G.* Sodium. *H.* Specific Conductance.

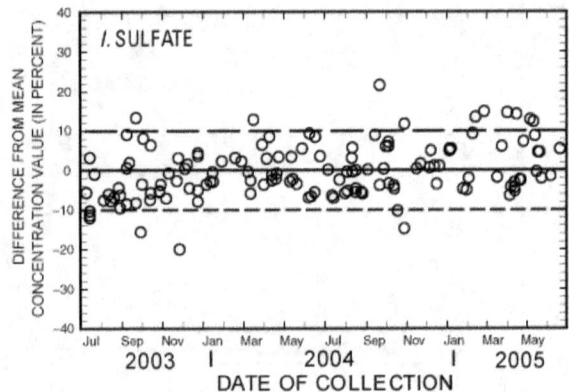

Figure 5. Blind reference sample results (continued): *I.* Sulfate.

For more information concerning this report, contact

Director
U.S. Geological Survey
New York Water Science Center
425 Jordan Road
Troy, NY 12180-8349
dc_ny@usgs.gov

or visit our Web site at:
http://ny.water.usgs.gov

≋USGS

Lincoln and others—Quality-Assurance Data for Routine Water Analyses by the Laboratory in Troy, New York—July 2003 through June 2005—Open-File Report 2009–1233